# Regression & Ritual, Family & Fatigue

Writings from my life
as an Indian
and my wildest dreams,
and letting down my guard
to reveal some nasty
little family secrets

by anand
with additional illustrations
by bernarda saldo
and friends

FUTURA HOUSE

Library of Congress Cataloging-in-Publication Data
Stratton, Mary-Margaret (anand sahaja)
Regression & Ritual, Family & Fatigue

Summary: "Writings from my life as an Indian and my wildest dreams, and letting down my guard to reveal some nasty little family secrets. A reminder to anyone who has been raised in a dysfunctional family (anyone out there?) that you are not alone. We live on a shadowed planet full of mysteries and lessons to learn. You can rise above it by expressing feelings in positive creative ways. Explore the arts... Survive and heal... This work expands beyond my normal life experience, whether from dreams, illusions, or transcendental fragmentary hypnotic moments. We all should walk a mile in someone else's moccasins." – Provided by the publisher.

ISBN-13: 978-0-9998749-6-7
ISBN-10: 0-9998749-6-7
1. Literature and Fiction >

Published by Futura House
2620 South Maryland Parkway #345
Las Vegas, NV 89109
Printed in the United States of America
www.futurahouse.com
Book Design and Images by MM Stratton (megorama.com)
using American Typewriter

# table of contents

## dedication

to the muses of charles bukowski
and sylvia plath.
to jeanne farrens.
and to my extended ACA family.

## fore-words

Gentle reader, this is a reminder to anyone who has been raised in a dysfunctional family that you are not alone. Nor have you ever been. We live on a shadowed planet full of mystery and lessons to learn. You can rise above it and reach the heavens by expressing feelings in positive creative ways.

Explore the arts...
Survive and heal...

This work expands beyond my normal life experience, whether from lucid dreams, momentary illusions, or transcendental and fragmentary hypnotic moments.

We all should walk a mile in someone else's moccasins.

# Fare Well Idaho

long black braids
swing
in your arms

as you lift me
high
we laugh

and quiet
for a moment
the still air surrounds

then the dry wind
carries away your thoughts
my one

serious your eyes
overwhelm me
with a feeling

you hold me
with the intensity
of never letting go.

# **Wistful**

Isabella fills me with longing
For warm wet afternoons
gray pensive skies
weighted low overhead
but just out of reach.

We've been here before.

She sings as if
someone else's smile
is hidden behind her,
another life inside,
just beyond
the mist gray of her eyes
and closeness
of close days.

ocean waves won't quench
the longing.
wistfully wishing
for I know not what.

# **Played out**

What comes after
this moment in time?
A handful of memories
and forgotten lines?
What will i find?
What will be mine?
When the stage is cleared
of the sets of the show?
A fondness for few
That i came to know?
Did I grow?
Now where do I go?

# **frustration**

the words are choked
to the back of my throat,
stuck there scratching
and many more churning
in my stomach,
rioting in my head,
and suffocating my chest.
I try to throw them all up.
Except the ones caught
in my internal organs
malignantly attached
to the vulnerable tissue,
growing tumorously
inside my feelings

truth

# Working My Tail Off

What does a day off feel like?
Even when I while away from working
The obsession never really goes away.
my mind makes long lists,
my muse is on vacation,
why aren't I?

What does life feel like?
I am overwhelmed beyond overwhelmed
with things to do to make life picture perfect.
Been running for so long
I've aged and worn my cells down
to the bone.

What does rest feel like?
My head is lop sided with left brain thinking.
My neck and shoulders are rock solid,
my lung muscles won't relax,
my jaws are tight from too many
bites and pulls,
chasing the tail of success.

# insomnia

eyelids open
paper hits the pavement.
the sound crows dawn
too many times
to count.

awake I am.
dead to the world.
dead to myself.

sleep avoids me
avoids the room
except mornings
and afternoons
and anytime
I am expected
to be awake.

# <u>Maha Gone</u>

offering peace and plenty,
but left ignored and
angered by ignorance,
the true proud
mahogany american
stands stern and frowning
by the door
of the cigar shop.

# Bright River

my son
Bright River
He grows up so quickly
sparkling with energy
in my eyes
reflecting the
sun.

balancing on a rock
he pushes coarse black hair
back from his eyes.

the river chuckles
with my young man.
his roundish hands
reach for shiny gray stones
that he shows to me
at end of the day.
his eyes glistening as
he leaves them on the earthen floor
to dry to dull memories.

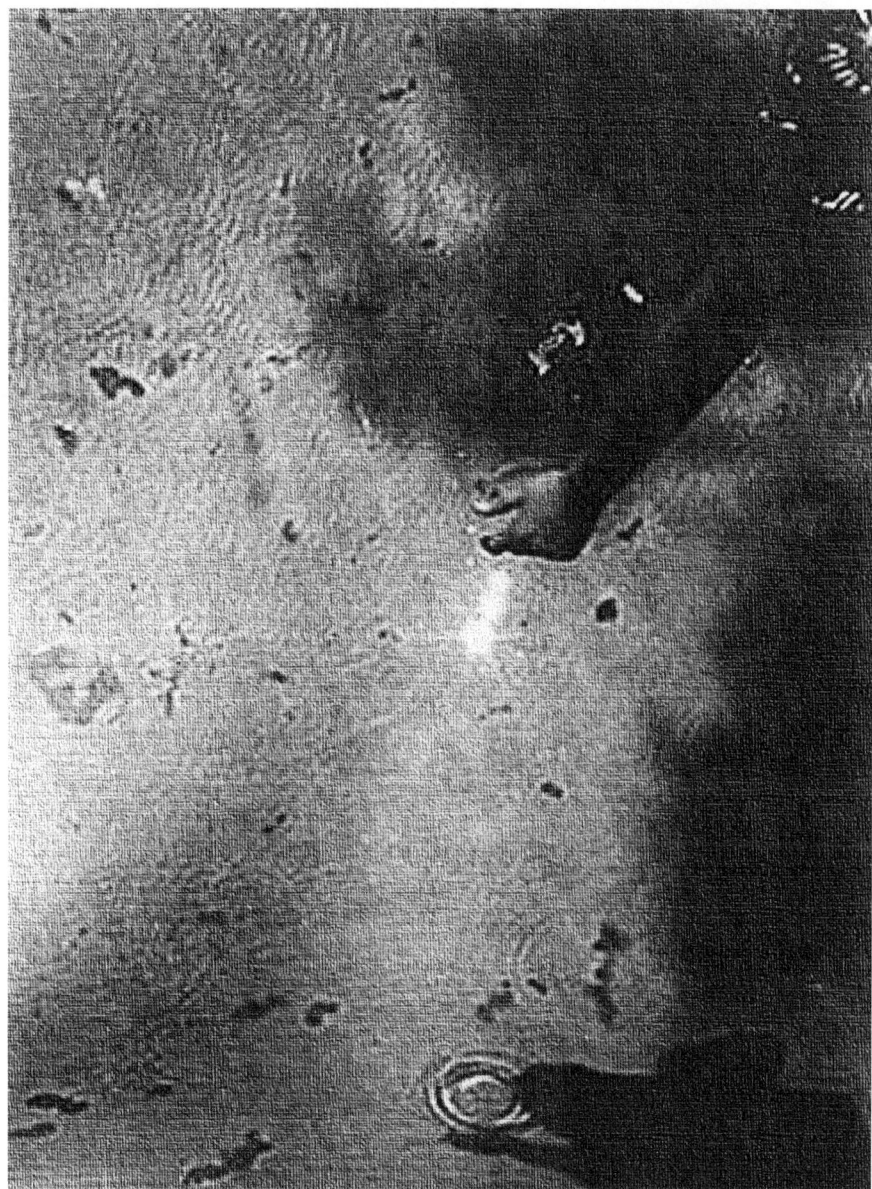

# wigwam haiku

desert cool
seeps through the
woven walls

# Night Thunder

Veiled in clouded thoughts
Lightening tongue struck me down.
His rage rumbled through my room.

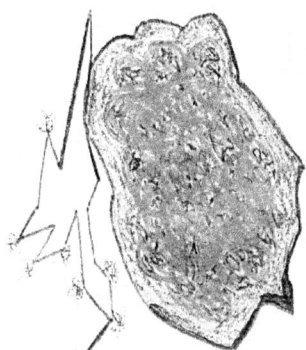

# the east wind

whirling clouds of dust and haze
trees prostrate to the ground
the great god wind has come.
it is Santana.

we try to turn away.
turn away,
but forcibly he reminds all
there is no place to hide.

harsh hot hands
easily penetrate my veil
and the omniscient god
pushes all
to bow down.

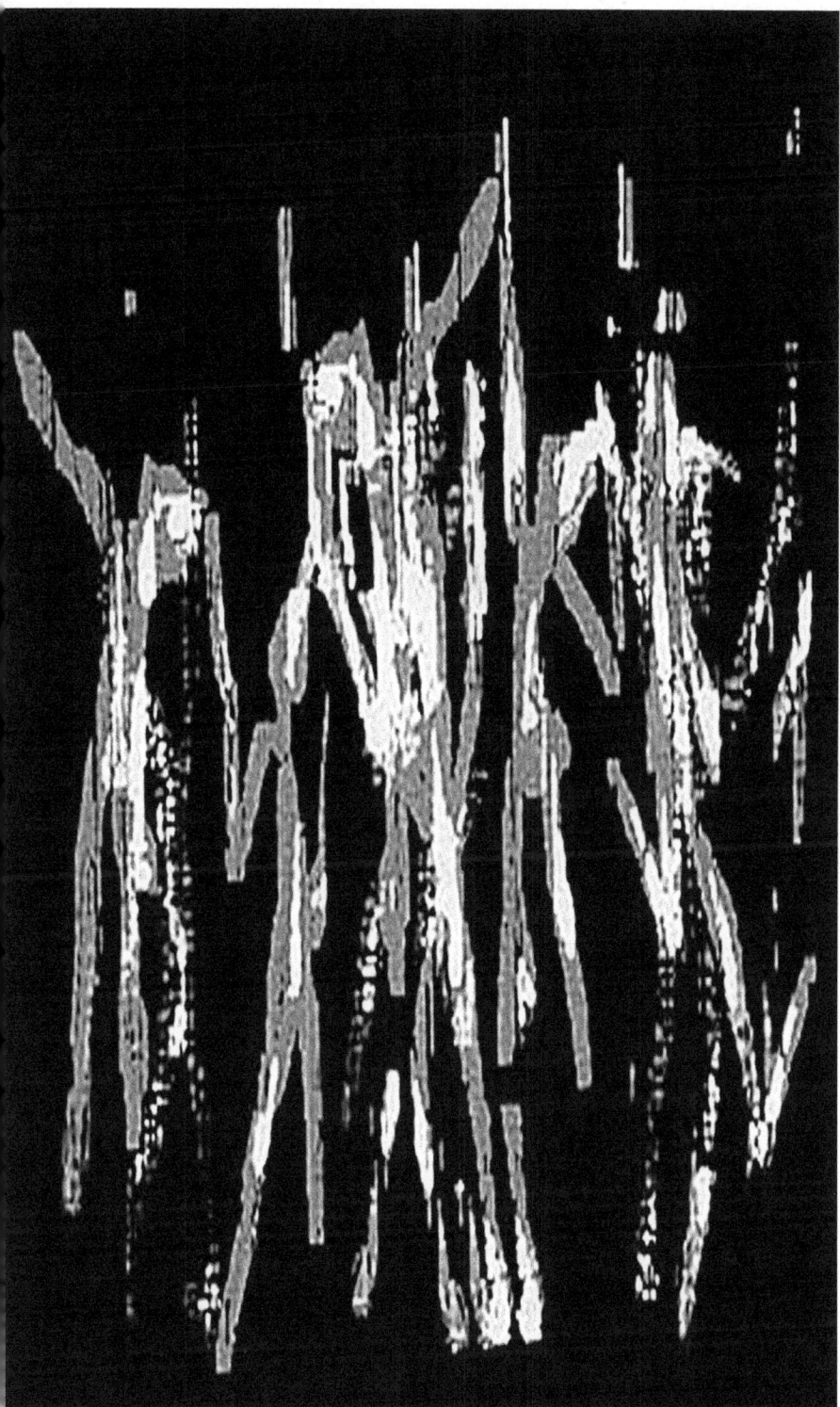

# long hall

look to the left
down the long hall.

grey blue florescents
light up.
glass doors reflect
cold old moldy walls,
and muffle the
reverberation
of studied sound.

many hours will be spent
biding time
looking down the long hall.

many doors will open.
many doors will close.

feet shuffle past
voices and noise
while I'm sitting still
on early evenings
working for a slip of paper
to frame on my wall.

it's going to be
a long haul.

# **daddy**

daddy why can't i remember
ever wanting to hug you
You held me once
you did.
you did.
so tight one afternoon
i blocked it out of my mind for years
but i know it happened
the pain of mama clutching me hard
so you couldn't

daddy daddy you do not love me?

you had a brown belt
the kind you still wear
i couldn't sit down for weeks

now i still can't sit still
so i found others like you
but no one has as big a belt as you

heal me
daddy
hug me.

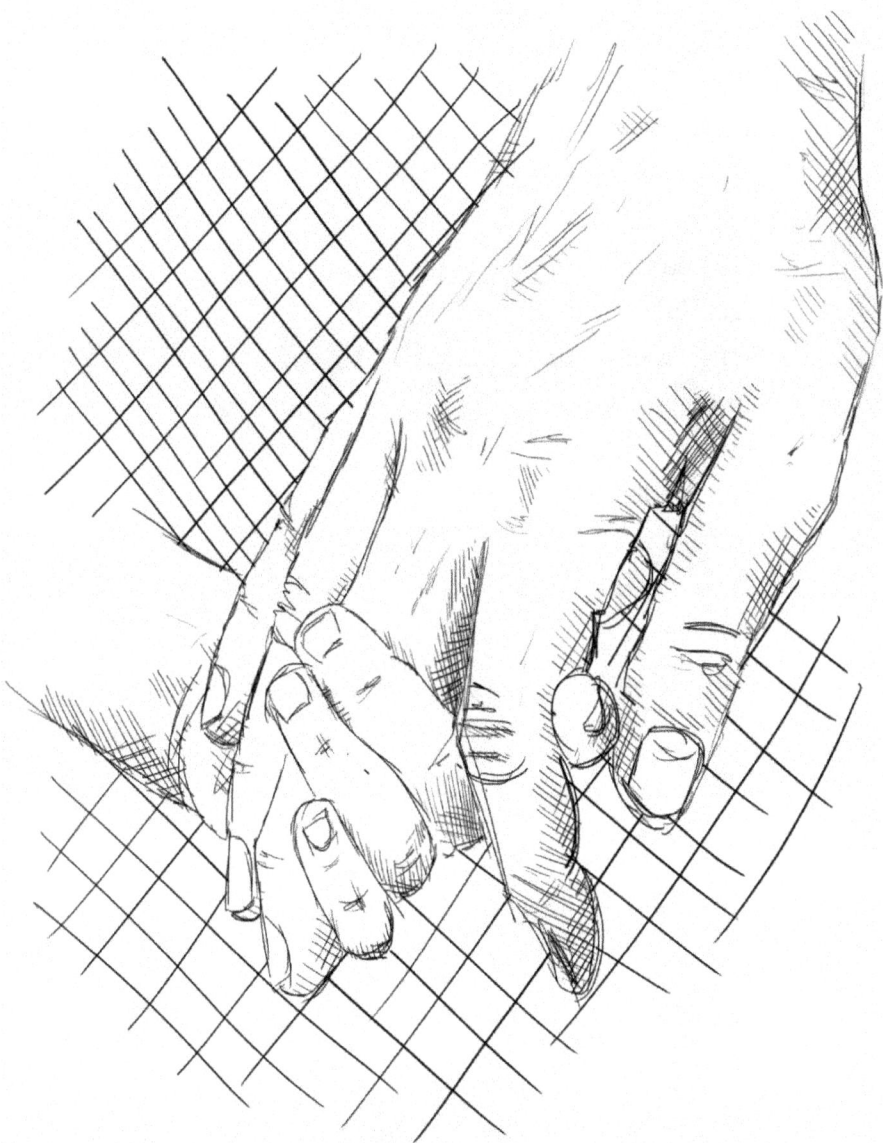

# Winkin

Winkin' and
Blinkin' and
Nod
stayed awake,
'cause they went
to a party
and came home
real late.
They went out
to breakfast
and dined on
Swiss steak.
Now the three
little souls
have a big
tummy ache.

# abu

abu is the man who
kills the desert crawler
on his belly in a striped shirt
and bells on his back.
he sheds the shirt and
the rattles give him away.

abu is the man who
kills the desert crawler
clawed to the ground on fours
and horns on his head.
he jerks and scatters and
the horns stand out from a cloud of dust.

abu is the man who
kills the desert crawler
upright, yet sluggish and slow
and a white painted face.
the fibers round his legs deprive
and the ghost white becomes real.

# **fatigue**

it makes one
go for the guttural

at some point
in the morning,
evening,
whatever...
things get punchy...
primitive.

the essential
factors of life
are laid bare:
to piss
to play
to provoke

and finally
one finds
fatigue quite
funny.

# **desert moon**

me:
purple silks and
incense and bells,
shimmering
gold and hair

him:
heavy head with
revelry and wine,
but alone
many women

here:
scent of musk and
gritty cold sand,
very cold
'tween my toes

up:
shining over
crystal naval
in the belly
of the sky

# my falcon

my falcon flies
and glides with great long strokes.
I learn from him
to guide my canoe
along the still deep waterways.

my falcon swoops
and ducks between the clouds.
I learn from him
to run through the trees
and navigate the rocky terrain.

my falcon dives
and chooses his prey
with deadly precision.
I learn from him

# L.A. Sky

yellow neon disk shines
behind the hole cut out
of gray construction paper.

        the sun coughed
        up blood today.
        choked by the
        steel tower's breath
        it fainted from the sky
        to the edge of the earth
        and heaved its final darkness
        at mankind.

# flapper

heavy beads above the ankles
velvet hat below the eyes
rose dust lingers on her dresser
a potpourri of lover's lies.
she lives her tiffany life of dreams
looking through colored glasses
and in shines a world of
beautiful hues where...
time of regret never passes.

# new orleans

free form jazz
playing about the place.
musical notes intertwining
around the brass railings
three stories high.
bright greens scent the air with
old perfume, and French food,
while the black man in the white suit
chatters away to the
boom boom bouncing bass.

# contrast

a bright open field
the sounds of children playing
with make believe bows and arrows
the men work hard tilling the soil
and harvesting the crops
a cat listens to the approaching sound of
hooves on the road
a cool fresh breeze blows
through the nearby trees.

civilization
the sound of a defenseless woman screaming
as a man threatens her with a gun
the men in their large stone structures
cheat each other to gain money and power
a dog lies dead in the street after a
passing car passed too fast
the thick stale smog makes it difficult to see
the dying trees.

## rosary

full bloody moon shines
through the window
ghostly like the picture
of virgin mary on the wall.
the woman in the sky
illuminates the face of a
dead religion.

# mater shed

bark brittle
broken off from the tree
you are nothing but splinters.

# Mrs. Gryson

how ya doing Mrs. Gryson?
i've a lot to say to you
'bout the little things you do.
what's the word that you've been saying
to the folks who pay the check?
can you sleep well at night knowing
all the little lives you'll wreck?

took a lot of time to figure out
and remember what you did
but it came back in a flash of shame
in memories well hid.
here's another thing to ponder
as I look back at your lies.
is there someone else to blame
for this sin that I despise?

hey hey hey Mrs. Gryson,
you've been playing in my mind,
and the thoughts I have aren't kind.
what the hell were you doing?
you were playing in my bed.
and i didn't know what for.
now I want to know you're dead.

you're a ruthless ruth
with a hole in your soul,
trampling innocent truth.
i hope you go to hell.

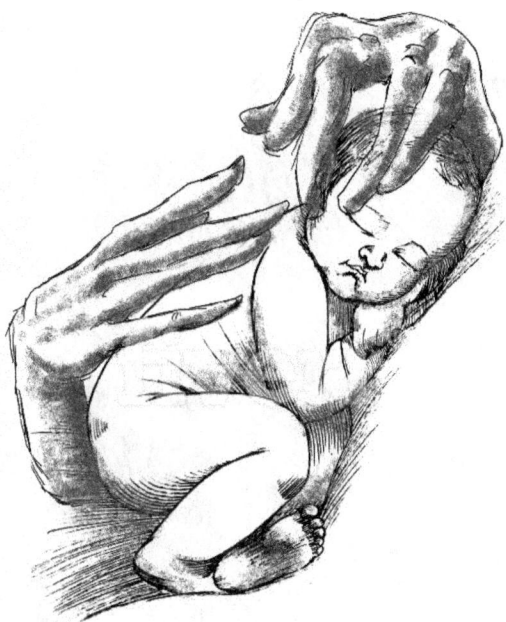

# Buddha Cries

My joy is to sing sweetly
and free-form dance
where no one can hear...
To sit on a shag cushion
and get drunk with friends
on a Saturday night...
Laughing and screaming
"Free man in the mornin,"
like Lonesome Rhodes
'til our throats ache;
Certainly not to sit in a 4x4 cell in squalor
awaiting certain murder by a
homicidal psychotic.

The catfish's Joy is to sulk around
at the bottom of a muddy bed,
feeling the tidal flow lift his fins,
slurping away at the briny algae,
exploring and spawning in the river deep;
Certainly not to hover and quiver
in a questionably unclear
two foot tank
with a watchful eye
at every passer-by
wondering who will carry the knife
to end his life.

The blue callinectes Joy
is to do the two-step, side-step
and click click click his claws
looking this way and that...
A nibble of mollusk here and there;
Certainly not to travel Auschwitz style
to end up at the Asian supermarket:
Thrown upside hither
in a tangled mass of his brethren
trying to wiggle unsuccessfully
to upright position,
only to be picked up by god tongs
and thrown back down again
by a godless woman.

# Geronimo

*(For Geronimo Pratt)*

Driving down my 60's ford.
You know I can get so bored.
With changing minds and no place to go.
Unfaithful kinds and the anger below.

Black shadow 'gainst the dusky sky,
Locked away for other's lies.
The 20 years has been unkind.
The fires burn on in my mind.

But knowledge does not come for free.
The psychic numbness beckons me.
The things I know are all untrue.
They're lean-to faces, then there's you.

Decorated, hanging gold.
The fear amassed and hearts grew cold.
Will we ever see the day
The front will pass and blow away?

Now you're gone and all is dust.
Next gen does what it thinks it must.
It's all illusion: black and white...
Would you condone
this fictitious fight?

# fucker

My father hasn't copulated in years
I know he hasn't.
My parent never kiss
sleep in separate beds
at opposite ends of the house.
He gives half-hearted hugs
to loved ones.

He seems much
too honorable
to be unfaithful
or to buy it on the street.
unless
his violent tendencies
drove him to rape?
No, I don't think so.
I mean...
He can be a mean old fucker
But he just doesn't, you know,
fuck.

# Whiskey Dreams

Head is heavy against
Sear's finest blend
Mind sluggish
Foot releasing the last bit
Of body energy.

I begin my whiskey dreams
Where every night
is a movie of the week,
On an endless car chase
Where brakes never work,
A spy thriller
Of global proportions.
Strange people
Become my friends,
And nothing goes as it should.

Where I do most of my living.

# Mother Mercy

You say you want to die
Sweet little elder child
So very vulnerable.
I come up behind
And hug those fragile shoulders
And squeeze
So much love I need to impart to you

The feelings well up in my throat
As I pull out your destiny
While my other arm wraps protectively
Around you.

You say you want to die
Over and over and over
Before you're senile.
Shoulders slump.

"Don't worry now.
You worry too much, mama.
Aren't you happier now?"

## mad man

he's flat-lined his feelings
for so long that
nothing can rile him.

now he reaches out in
typed words emailing
mechanical love

slow day slow day          oh nothing, just a slow day slow day

slow day slow day

slow day slow day

slow day slow day

# To begin with

I should like to strangle my mother

who warps and distorts
everything around her,
is so screwed up
in her thoughtful thinking
(which she does
every single second of
her drawn out life)

If I did choke her
feel my hands closing
around her sagging old throat
then maybe the distasteful
resent-filled meanness in her
would stay stuck inside.

THAT is what will
ultimately kill her
in the end.

# **doldrums**

no wind in my sails
afloat and adrift
unanchored,
yet unsinking,
passing from
past life to present
as time passes away

# clock critique

when the electric alarm clock breaks
it's harder to get up in the morning.
the gentle little hum is gone,
replaced by the loud tick-tocking:
drudgery,
monotony,
with persistent dedication
to marching forward,
and an annoying loyalty
to an oppressive future.

When you can't hear time,
it seems more benign.

But this alarm clock...
a totally inaccurate device.
needing constant care,
winding and setting.
and always always moving
much too fast.

# Grandma Vicks

you smell of dusty dried roses,
death and grandpa's funeral.
you marinate in yesterdays
and aggrieved sufferings.
you lie buried in bed clothes
and sickly medicines.

please arise and ascend
so you can live again.

# Reflection

My mother's shadow
reflects in the sliding glass

it is dark and unlike the dancer
who once listened to dreams,
gave goodnight hugs,
and late night glass of water.

the light hovers by her shoulder.
it illuminates her escapist novel.

the reflection of darkness is kind
to the graying tresses,
age spots and wrinkles
and empty eyes
cannot be seen.

# chronic infestation

i banish him
over and over
from my presence,

and yet he still manages to
ooze on down
through the back door.
Foggy, slimy, slippery,
filled with deceit and falsehood,
and fathomed up by fear.

for the neophyte of light
it is paramount to
wax on.
wax off.
wax on.
wax off.
wax on.
wax off.

be ever ready.
and
keep up
your spiritual dukes.

YOU MAY HAVE TO BE
PATIENT NOW - THINK, LISTEN
AND HEED SIGNS.

WATCH
OUT

# derricks

silhouetted against
a charcoal amber sunset,
their shadows stretch
across the
burnt landscape.
giant mosquitos
on the hills
sucking the life blood
out of the earth.

# satan's makin' babies

the "christians" are clueless.
they fight against roe v. wade,
with vim and vigor,
never realizing
the divine plan
of YahWah.

they are being saved
from being overrun
by demonic plague.

the results of rape,
an immoral age,
and mindless, love-less
fornication
are not the highest choice
for creating babies,
but it is a perfect way
to give Jezebel a porthole.

if ALL is His will and His way,
then liberating the unclean seed
could very well Be His Strategy.

have some faith people.

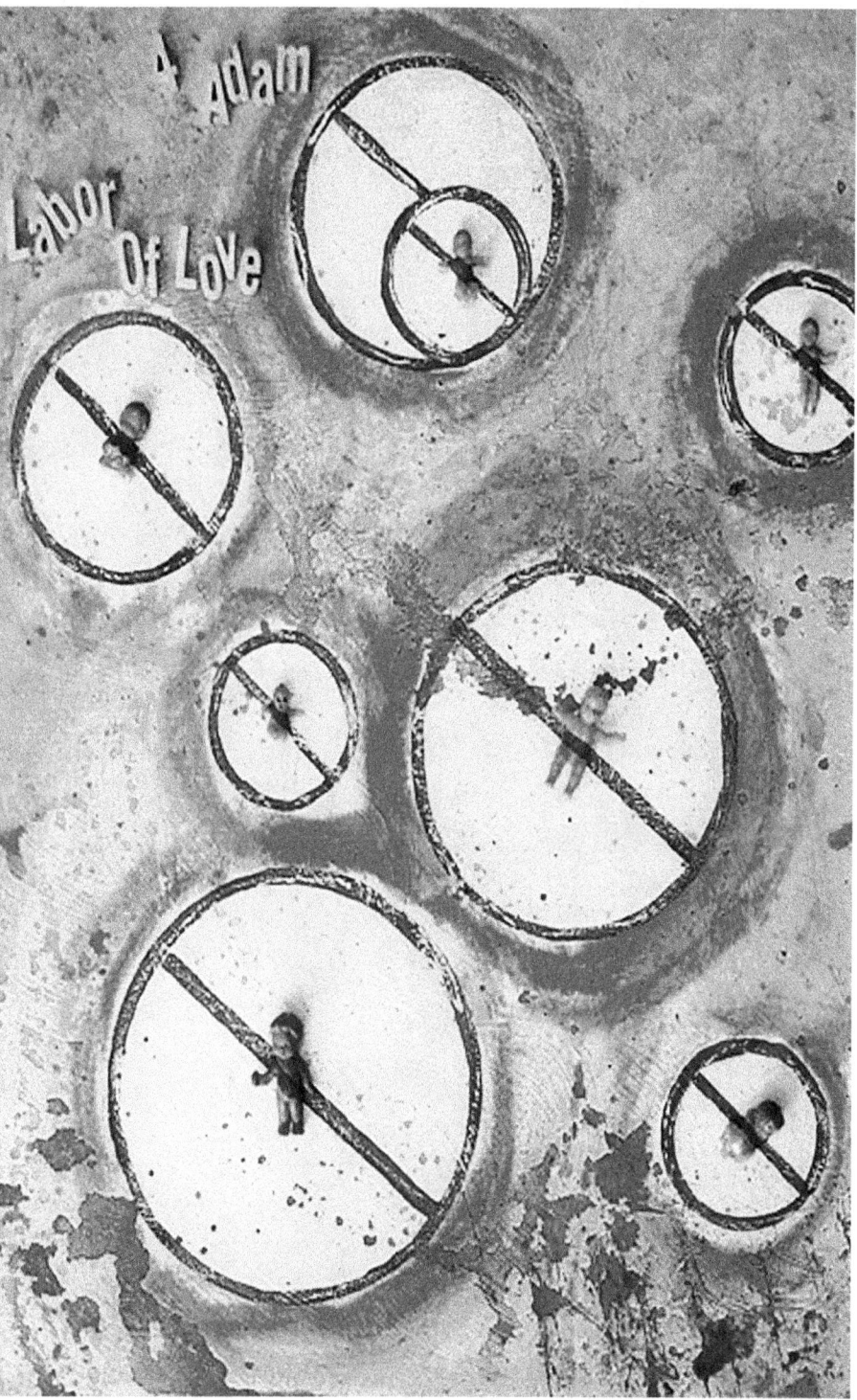

4 Adam

Labor
Of Love

# high as a kite

head swamp
murky and muddled
mental conditions
dissolve away
with the ease of a
"fantastic" commercial.
one mind wipe
and
i soar upward
on my life string
above all the
dingy distress.

# Mother

I HATE YOU
You are an unhappy
jealous woman
And your life has not
turned out as you hoped.
So you try to make me feel
smaller than a flea.
Squeeze me
and try to squash me,
but my shell is hard
and I will jump
away from you...

Away where I can remember
good things about you
when you held me as a child
and taught me that I
possessed the power
to defend myself.
You made me feel
I could do anything.
and for that
i love you.

## stoned

you built your wall
of cold bricks
worn around the edges
graying with age.
hysterically
i try to get through,
but my fist
meets hard stone,
cemented down firmly,
yet decaying in denial
and crumbling in time.

# GUILTY

forgiven and yet not forgotten.
i made peace
with my parent's guilty past.

for the things they were culpable of:
dysfunction junction,
beatings, harassment,
abuse, bully tactics,
isolation and
emotional abandonment,
despicable criticism,
self-pity and
insufferable judgement.

now i have come full circle
to feel sorrow
for their lost opportunities,
to see their weakness reflected in me,
to love them despite their faults.
i wish i had taken time,
tried to understand THEM better.

now, i am the one who feels
guilty.

# about the author~illustrator

anand has been published
by Westwind - UCLA's
Journal of the Arts,
Manuscript Magazine,
Seventeen Magazine, and
other journals of creative
writing. She enjoys writing
short and punchy,
irreverent and insightful
poetry and prose. By day she is a professional
creative communications consultant. By night,
a musician and artist. She longs to spend a year
in Paris painting, and a year in Manhattan
painting the town.

anandsahaja.com

## other works by anand:

Non Fiction

Dominant Health
Eat Like Eve
The Good Wiccan Guides
How Modern Was
  My Valley
Kiss Addiction Goodbye
Kiss Addiction Away
Marry & Grow Happy
Mondo Vegas
Pop Tags – Volumes 1&2
Stop Picking on Me
SPOM Workbook
The SoLa SoFiA Method

Fiction/Prose

Endings?
An Heirloom Adventure
My Life As An Angel
One Toy, Two Toys, Too
  Many Shoo Toys
Please Don't Eat My
  Friends
Sex & Single Girl
  Revisited
Wheel of the Year
Why Am I?

# about the illustrator

Bernarda Saldo hails from Croatia. She likes coffee, dogs, South Park, sunsets and bread, in no particular order! She is a trained illustrator and especially loves to work in the black and white mode in both an abstract and literal style. She feels, "There is a special bond between poetry and illustration."

Instagram: crtamito

~ pages 7, 9, 15, 21, 27, 29, 33, 34, 37, 53, 57, 63, 65, 80, 89

# additional illustrators

Alen Burazerovic is an illustrator and animator from Bosnia & Herzegovina with an MFA in printmaking. Instagram/alenburazerovic ~ pages 39, 59, 90

Cary Brian Stratton aka Chef Mason Green is an accomplished musical performer and artist CaryStratton.com ~ pages 23, 41, 46

Fred Haro aka 'Suicide Sam' is a Southern California artist and animator ~ page 68

Marko Atanacković is a Serbian illustrator with a Masters in Fine Art from the University of Belgrade. ~ pages 54, 57

Michael Palumbo is a New York based exhibit designer whose credits include Imagineering and the California Science Center ~ page 31

Natalie Pace "Davis Stirring Up Stars in the Denoff Pool." ©Natalie Pace. Co-creator of the Earth Gratitude project and bestselling author of The Gratitude Game, The ABCs of Money and Put Your Money Where Your Heart Is. NataliePace.com ~ page 19

Oksana Didkova is an ink and watercolor artist from the Ukraine ~ pages 49, 51

Poulomi Mondal has a degree in graphic design from St. Xavier's College in India facebook/skylantern23 ~ page 53

Yastrebova Tanya is from Russia and her favorite illustration style is watercolor. Instagram/iva_nova_8 ~ pages 71, 85

Thank you for listening.

www.ingramcontent.com/pod-product-compliance
Lightning Source LLC
Chambersburg PA
CBHW071056040426
42443CB00013B/3357